GEARED FOR GROWTH BIBLE STUDIES
UNSHAKEABLE CONFIDENCE
A STUDY IN HABAKKUK & JOEL

BIBLE STUDIES TO IMPACT THE LIVES
OF ORDINARY PEOPLE

Christian Focus Publications

The Word Worldwide

Written by A. Bakes

PREFACE
GEARED FOR GROWTH

'Where there's LIFE there's GROWTH: Where there's GROWTH there's LIFE.'

WHY GROW a study group?

Because as we study and share the Bible together we can

- learn to combat loneliness, depression, staleness, frustration, and other problems
- get to understand and love each other
- become responsive to the Holy Spirit's dealing and obedient to God's Word

and that's GROWTH.

How do you GROW a study group?

- Just ask by asking a friend to join you and then aim at expanding your group.
- Study the set portions daily (they are brief and easy: no catches).
- Meet once a week to discuss what you find.
- Befriend others, both Christians and non Christians and work away together

see how it GROWS!

WHEN you GROW ...

This will happen at school, at home, at work, at play, in your youth group, your student fellowship, women's meetings, mid-week meetings, churches and communities,

you'll be REACHING THROUGH TEACHING

HABAKKUK and JOEL

INTRODUCTORY STUDY

CONFIDENCE IN GOD

God promised: 'My Presence will go with you' (Exod. 33:14).
Moses said: 'If your Presence does not go with us, do not send us not up from here' (Exod. 33:15).
David sang: 'With God we shall gain the victory' (Ps. 60:12).
John wrote: 'God is greater than our hearts, and he knows everything' (I John 3:20).

'I know who holds the future, and I know He holds my hand.'

Share thoughts from the above quotes in relation to:

    earthquakes,
      floods,
        collapsing governments,
          horrific accidents,
            birth abnormalities, etc.

In family life, most people find a sense of worth. For some, their position in a local community or place of employment enlarges this self-worth. For others, a position of authority in government or church gives even greater self-esteem.

However, during times of calamity, personal or national, the foundation of confidence is shaken, and frequently found inadequate. No easy remedy will succeed.

In circumstances like these it is important to know God the great creator, our Father, is never out of control. He is the immovable rock on which faith for a secure eternity can be built.

Habakkuk and Joel, the prophets we are about to study, both faced problems and found their confidence in Jehovah. They believed He was in control of the events of their day, and trusted Him for any unknown future calamities. Habakkuk affirmed his utter faith in God in his remarkable statement in Habakkuk 3:17-18. Joel, in his prophecy of the coming Day of Judgment against sin, was confident of salvation through God alone for all who call on His name.

How would you face up to a personal tragedy?

* your husband or wife leaving you;
* the death of a loved one;
* losing your job;
* finding that your child is on drugs;
* being told you have a terminal illness;
* having an accident which leaves you disabled.

These things are happening to people all the time. Would your confidence in God help you if tragedy struck your life? In what way?

All around us, people are hurting. Think of someone who is hurting. How can your confidence in God enable you to help them?

Share your ideas in the group, and decide to put some of them into practice this week.

BACKGROUND TO HABAKKUK

The date of writing was most probably between 605-589 BC in the reign of Jehoiakim, king of Judah, and Nebuchadnezzar of the Chaldeans or Babylonians (2 Kings 23:24-37; Jer. 22).

Just prior to the writing of Habakkuk, the nations around Judah were shocked by the overthrow of the Assyrian Empire and the Egyptians by the newly emerging power of King Nebuchadnezzar of Babylon. Throughout this period, Judah was caught up in religious and moral turmoil. The godly suffered harshly under the oppression of the ungodly.

The book of Habakkuk is valuable as a unique dialogue between the prophet and God. It is full of instruction concerning God as sovereign over nations and events (1:5; 2:13-17).

The prophet has a strong reaction to sin, for he knows God as the Holy One (1:2-4, 13a).

He calls to God for:
  Judgment of Judah's sins, and
  Judgment on the wickedness of the Babylonian enemy.

Both judgments eventually occurred. Judah was ransacked and the people exiled. Later, the Babylonian empire fell to the Persians in 539 BC. At that time the Jewish captive remnant were allowed to return to their native land.

The central theme of the book is in 2:4: 'The righteous will live by his faith'.

The theme is taken up in the New Testament in Romans 1:17; Galatians 3:11; Hebrews 10:38-39.

HABAKKUK

STUDY 1
THE PROPHET'S BURDEN

QUESTIONS

DAY 1 *Habakkuk 1:1-4.*
a) How is Habakkuk described in verse 1?
b) What particular forms of evil characterised the society in which Habakkuk lived? Do you see any modern day parallels?

DAY 2 *Habakkuk 1:2-4.*
a) How did Habakkuk react to the evil he saw around him?
b) What do you think he was wanting God to do? What apparently was not happening?

DAY 3 *Habakkuk 1:2.*
a) What characteristics of Habakkuk's prayer life are evident here.
b) A desperate cry to God ... no quick answer! What are we encouraged to do in Luke 11:1-10; Colossians 4:2?
c) Write out Jesus' words of encouragement to persevere in prayer from Matthew 7:7-8.

DAY 4 *2 Peter 2:4-10.*
a) From these events in the lives of Noah and Lot, discuss the ways in which God was in control.
b) God watches over His people today. Find the verse from the reading to support this promise.

DAY 5 *Habakkuk 1:5-6.*
a) Who now begins to speak in this verse?
b) What amazing thing was going to happen?

DAY 6 *Habakkuk 1:7-11.*
a) How are the Babylonians described?
b) What warning had been given in Deuteronomy 28:15,49-52. How would the Babylonians closely match this prophecy?

DAY 7 *Habakkuk 1:5-11.*
a) What did the Babylonians think about themselves (v. 11b)?
b) Who really was at work despite all that was going to happen (v. 5)?

NOTES

THE SETTING
The kingdom of Judah was undermined by backsliding,
Righteous people were in the minority, and were hemmed around by violence and strife (1:4).

HABAKKUK'S PROBLEM
The prophet was deeply concerned as he saw the terrible unfaithfulness of God's chosen nation, and the sinful behaviour which resulted. A heavy burden was on him because of the increasing spiritual apathy and the resulting violence (1:3). He had prayed and prayed!

THE PROPHET HANDLING HIS PROBLEM
Verses 2-4 bring us the cry of his aching heart as he calls out to God: 'How long, O LORD, must I call for help, but you do not listen?' His prayer is desperate and urgent.

Centuries earlier, while suffering as slaves in Egypt, the nation had sent up a similar prayer for help. Where could they turn, but to God? Exodus 2:23-25 records their urgent cry, and God's response.

SPECIFIC PRAYER RECEIVES SPECIFIC ANSWERS
God answers Habakkuk in 1:5-11, but not with the expected message of deliverance for the righteous, and judgment of the evildoers. Instead, He tells Habakkuk to look beyond Judah's boundaries to the army of Babylon that was to become His instrument of judgment against Judah (1:5).

A CHALLENGE TODAY
All around the world people disregard God, His Word and His ways. They are lost.

Can you sense God's burden for the unsaved? Will you become concerned for them, as Habakkuk was for Judah?

Ask God to increase your awareness of their hopelessness, and then pray for them.

STUDY 2
THE PROPHET IS PERPLEXED

QUESTIONS

DAY 1 *Habakkuk 1:2-4; Psalm 77.*
a) What similarities exist between the prayer of the psalmist and that of Habakkuk?
b) What did the psalmist do to resolve his doubts (vv. 10-12)? What could he declare about God?

DAY 2 *Habakkuk 1:12-13.*
a) Who is now speaking in these verses?
b) What characteristics of God are referred to here? Which one is prominent in verse 13?

DAY 3 *Habakkuk 1:6,12-13.*
a) Genesis 6:5; Psalm 11:4; Hebrews 4:13. What are we reminded about God in these verses?
b) In the light of these verses, what do you think Habakkuk meant when he said that God's eyes were too pure to look on evil?

DAY 4 *Habakkuk 1:13-17.*
a) How does the prophet describe the Babylonians? What did he complain to God about?
b) Psalm 73:3-12. How does this description of the wicked match that of the Babylonians given in Habakkuk 1:13-17? What caused the psalmist to later change his mind about the wicked (Ps. 73:16-20)?

DAY 5 *Habakkuk 2:1* (read in as many translations as possible).
a) To whom does Habakkuk compare himself with? What was he expecting from God?
b) What does Psalm 130 and Hebrews 11:6 say about prayer? Do we expect answers when we pray?

DAY 6 *Habakkuk 2:1-3.*
a) How long did Habakkuk have to wait before God answered him?
b) What did God say about the revelation He would give him?
c) What was Habakkuk to do with it?

QUESTIONS (contd.)

DAY 7 *Habakkuk 2:4-5.*
 a) Who are contrasted in these verses?
 b) What important statement is repeated in Galatians 3:11?
 c) What does Romans 3:20-24 teach us about righteousness and faith?

NOTES

THE SETTING
God has answered the anguished cry of the prophet who is surrounded by decadent living. God has opened his eyes to see the treacherous Babylonian army whom He will use to deal with His sinful people.

THE MAN OF GOD IS SHOCKED
This revelation stuns Habakkuk. Although he hates Judah's sin and neglect of God, he is grieved that many good people must also suffer at the hands of the foe. His original problem is compounded.

The picture of Judah's inhabitants, like fish swimming aimlessly with no regard for God as ruler, is awful enough. But to see the enemy enclosing them in their nets and growing rich and proud at their expense, is devastating. Habakkuk wonders how a holy God can allow evil to triumph over righteousness.

HANDLING HIS PROBLEM
So, almost with indignation, he cries out to God again. He acknowledges the Lord's holiness and sovereignty, but questions the severity of the punishment through men evil enough to sacrifice to the weapons of their warriors.

Then in chapter 2:1, he becomes quiet, and settles down to wait for God's reply.

GOD'S SPECIFIC ANSWER
In His mercy God does not rebuke Habakkuk, but assures him that 'the just will live by his faith'.

The coming message must be written very clearly so that everyone can read it with understanding, and then pass it on. God explains that the message is about future events that will happen at His appointed time.

THE CHALLENGE TODAY
Uncertainties, delays and misunderstandings can cause depression and fear. The writer of Psalm 77 cried to God out of his depression, and was uplifted as he meditated on God's holy ways.

Is your knowledge of God increasing through the reading of His Word? Faith will grow, and we can echo David's words: 'He will judge the world in righteousness, he will govern the peoples with justice ... Those who know your name will trust in you, for you, Lord, have never forsaken those who seek you' (Ps. 9:8, 10).

STUDY 3
GOD SPEAKS

QUESTIONS

DAY 1 *Habakkuk 2:4.*
a) How were the righteous to live through difficult times? Were they promised an easy passage?
b) Psalm 11. What did the psalmist do when he was attacked? Do you believe God is still on the throne where you live?

DAY 2 *Habakkuk 2:5-8.*
a) Mark 7:20-23. What was the root cause of the sins Jesus lists here? Which of these sins were being practised by the Babylonians?
b) How would the Babylonians be judged? Can you think of more recent examples of oppressed people revolting against their oppressors?

DAY 3 *Habakkuk 2:9-13.*
a) To what limits were the Babylonians prepared to go to obtain success? Would their success be temporal or eternal?
b) Isaiah 55:1-3; John 4:7-14. From where is true, lasting satisfaction to be found?

DAY 4 *Habakkuk 2:14; Psalm 86:9; 102:15; Isaiah 52:10,15.*
a) What theme do these verses have in common?
b) Romans 10:11-15. How will this purpose of God for the nations be fulfilled?

DAY 5 *Habakkuk 2:15-17*
a) The Babylonians had induced others to drunkenness. How would the tables now be turned on them?
b) Matthew 26:36-46. What cup did the Lord Jesus drink for us?

DAY 6 *Habakkuk 2:18-19.*
a) Why are idols described as worthless?
b) Romans 1:18-25. How is the decline in man's sinful behaviour explained here?

QUESTIONS (contd.)

DAY 7 *Habakkuk 2:20; Psalm 33:6-11; 89:5-8.*
 a) What should inspire silence before God?
 b) Glance through this chapter again. What glimpses did Habakkuk get of God, and how would it have encouraged him?

NOTES

THE SETTING
God explains in detail His justice concerning the cruel nation of Babylon. In the end, wickedness will not win over righteousness. This is the essence of the vision, or answer, which Habakkuk is to write plainly.

Although its fulfilment may seem slow in coming, God promises that it will definitely take place. The people must wait for it (2:2-3).

PROPHECY IN DETAIL
It is true that Judah will suffer for their rebellion, but the sin and pride of Babylon will be dealt with also. God issues a series of five warnings against the enemy:

You stole and plundered. You will be robbed in return (2:6-8).
You are condemned for destroying many nations, and will face retaliation (vv. 9-11).
You built cities on crime. They will come to nothing (vv. 12-13).
You degraded your neighbours. You yourselves will be shamed (vv. 15-17).
You trust in man-made idols, which are completely useless (vv. 18-19).

IDOLS ARE POWERLESS
The final warning, pointing out the futility of calling on idols for deliverance, presents a stark contrast. A god made of wood or stone is visible, but lifeless. But the true God is alive, long-suffering, all-seeing, all-knowing and reigning. He is the one to be worshipped with reverence.

GOD WILL BE WORSHIPPED
The Lord's answer has finally satisfied Habakkuk's questioning heart. We, too, can take comfort. Look again at 2:13, 14, 20. These verses assure us that God, who is almighty, all-powerful, all-glorious and sovereign, has a plan for the climax of the ages when the earth will be filled with the knowledge of His glory. What a basis for praise and worship here and now!

Following the description of the uselessness of idols we have the moving verse: 'But the Lord is in his holy temple, let all the earth be silent before him' (2:20). In our noisy world it is good to ponder on God's holiness and His presence, and to worship Him in silence as a token of our submission to His power. In the future, nations and men of rank will be stunned to silence as the sovereign God demonstrates His absolute control over the affairs of the world.

CHALLENGE FOR TODAY
What can I do to hasten the spread of the knowledge of the glory of God throughout the world? Have I five minutes today in which to think about the greatness of my God?

STUDY 4
A STATEMENT OF FAITH

QUESTIONS

DAY 1 *Habakkuk 3:1-2.*
a) From the first and last sentences in this chapter, in what way was this prayer most likely offered to God?
b) What was Habakkuk's request in verse 2? On what basis did he appeal to God? How does Hebrews 4:15-16 encourage us to pray?

DAY 2 *Habakkuk 3:3-4.*
a) What event may Habakkuk have been thinking about as he penned these words (Exod 19:16-20; 20:18; 24:15-17)?
b) According to John 1:1,14, how was God's glory later revealed?

DAY 3 *Habakkuk 3:5-15.*
a) What other events in Israel's history might Habakkuk have been thinking about as he tried to describe God's majesty?
b) For whom did God display His power (v. 13)?

DAY 4 *Habakkuk 3:13-14.*
a) What similarities exist between God's victory here and the victory of Jesus over the devil on the cross (Gen. 3:14-15; John 14:30; 1 John 3:8)?
b) In what way was the victory of Habakkuk 3:14 dramatic?

DAY 5 *Habakkuk 3:16-19.*
a) What attitude did Habakkuk adopt as he waited on God?
b) 'It is not in our circumstances, but in the God of our salvation that we should rejoice.' Discuss this statement. Considering life around you, write a prayer in modern day language similar to the one in 3:17-18.

DAY 6 *Habakkuk 3:16-19.*
a) Why might Habakkuk have wanted his feet to be like that of a deer or hind? How would he achieve this?
b) Ephesians 1:4-6. Where is a Christian said to dwell?

QUESTIONS (contd.)

DAY 7 *Habakkuk 1:2-4, 12-17.*
a) How are these two previous prayers of Habakkuk different from the one recorded in chapter 3?
b) How had Habakkuk moved from a state of questioning (1:2), to one of confidence and joy in God (3:18)?

NOTES

THE SETTING
Habakkuk stands between the past and the future.
   He remembers God's faithfulness to His people over previous centuries, and is encouraged to believe that His holiness and sovereignty will be seen at the end. Therefore he can pray confidently for God's power to be visibly active in his own day.

THE PAST
As one writer says: 'It is helpful to remember God's gracious working in the past. It encourages us in our present faith in the Lord and gives us confidence to face the future' (Goldsmith).
   A review of the wide-ranging glory of God is seen in the powerful display of 3:3-6. Then some of the past events showing God's power come to Habakkuk's mind in 3:7-15, including a reminder that His anger produced salvation (3:13). Similarly, we are reminded that God's reason for stepping into history in His Son was not to condemn, but to save (John 3:17).

THE PRESENT
As men and creation trembled before God's righteous anger in the past, Habakkuk confesses that he too quivers with fear on hearing God's prophecy. This physical trembling contrasts with the strength of his spirit. In remembering God's faithfulness to His people of old, he joyfully trusts the Lord for the present and the future.

CHALLENGE TODAY
On the one hand we face our circumstances, sometimes good and sometimes bad. On the other hand stands God's constant faithfulness.

   'Let us fix our eyes on Jesus, the author and perfecter of our faith, who for the joy set before him endured the cross, scorning its shame, and sat down at the right hand of the throne of God' (Heb. 12:2).

   Let us determine to plot a steady course in spite of circumstances, knowing that God has plans He is working out through our lives.
   To quote Goldsmith again: 'Rejoicing in the Lord, and in His gracious work of salvation, may be considered the true fulfilment of the life of faith'.

JOEL

BACKGROUND FOR JOEL

The name of this man of God means 'Jehovah is God'. From this we assume that his father was a true servant of Jehovah.

Joel recognised the word of the Lord when God gave him this message and prophecy for the kingdom of Judah.

It is uncertain when Joel lived and prophesied, but the truths of the book cover a wide time span from the actual locust plague to the coming Day of Judgment for the nations. It seems he was familiar with the term 'Day of the Lord' as used by other prophets in Isaiah 2:12, Amos 5:20, etc.

The message consists of two almost equal parts:

1:1–2:17   The locust plague, and the Day of the Lord, about which the prophet is speaking.
2:18–3:21   The victory to come, in which the Lord is speaking.

The turning point in the book comes at 2:18. The result of repentance is deliverance through the grace of Jehovah God, followed by His blessing.

Our study in this book, as in Habakkuk, will reinforce basic truths of the Christian faith. The joy of salvation from God's righteous judgment, through faith in Christ, will motivate us to share the gospel far and wide, with renewed confidence in God, our reigning King.

STUDY 5
THE PROPHET AND THE WORD

QUESTIONS

DAY 1 *Joel 1:1-7.*
a) What two facts about Joel are we made aware of in verse 1?
b) What was the background of his message from God?

DAY 2 *Joel 1:1-4; Psalm 78:1-8.*
a) What age group is addressed in verse 2? What were they to do?
b) What would be the value of passing on the facts of this event from one generation to another?

DAY 3 *Joel 1:5-7.*
a) Who were seemingly oblivious to the surrounding disaster?
b) Romans 13:11-14. How is a Christian to live?

DAY 4 *Joel 1:8-12; Leviticus 2:1-3; 23:12-14.*
a) Why were the priests mourning and what had caused this?
b) What contrast exists between Joel 1:12 and Habakkuk 3:17-18?

DAY 5 *Joel 1:13-14.*
a) Who all were to be involved in this national repentance?
b) What form was it to take?

DAY 6 *Joel 1:13-14.*
a) What does God promise in 2 Chronicles 7:13-15 and Jeremiah 29:13?
b) Is fasting relevant for us today (Matt. 6:16-18)?

DAY 7 *Joel 1:1,13-14; 2:1.*
a) Discuss the role that Joel played in the nation's repentance.
b) 2 Timothy 3:16-17. Why is it important for us to read and meditate on God's Word?

NOTES

THE SETTING
Joel, the man of God, receives the word of the Lord, and speaks it forth. So Joel's words are God's words firstly to Judah, and now to us.

THE PROPHECY
The prophecy is related to an unprecedented natural calamity. Never before had an event of such magnitude been recorded in the nation's history.

THE EVENTS
The land was totally devastated by a plague of locusts, insects with voracious appetites during their four stages of growth.

The inability to continue daily cereal and drink offerings was a dreadful side effect. These voluntary offerings were made to God in thanks for His goodness and provision. Because of the locusts there was now nothing to offer, and scarcely a reason for thanksgiving. Joel sees the locust invasion as a punishment for national sin, and calls for national repentance.

ACTION
Through Joel, God calls for action. He issues commands which, if followed, will lead to repentance: Awake! Lament! Mourn! Set aside a fast day!

Solomon once had a similar message from God for the nation: 'if my people who are called by my name, will humble themselves and pray ... then will I hear ... and will forgive their sin and will heal their land' (2 Chron. 7:14).

WORD OF LIFE
God's Word through the ages is straight and true. Today's Christians should use it as food for their souls, and for guidance in daily living. Through the Scriptures the Holy Spirit teaches and preserves the believer.

Jesus prayed that His Father would sanctify (set apart) His disciples through the Word, which is truth (John 17:17). We who follow Him today are set apart for Him through the same holy Word.

CHALLENGE
What value do I set on the written Word of God? Do I really care that some of God's people do not possess a copy of it?

Let's read and reread it! Listen to it! Obey it! Tell out its message as long as we live!

STUDY 6
REPENT! RETURN!

QUESTIONS

DAY 1 *Joel 1:13-16; Luke 11:1-4.*
a) How did Jesus teach His disciples to address God?
b) Pick out words about God in Joel 1:13-16 which show that He is a personal God.

DAY 2 *Joel 1:15-20.*
a) Apart from the locusts, what other catastrophes were the people experiencing? What effects of these are noted?
b) About what was the prophet particularly concerned (v. 15)?

DAY 3 *Deuteronomy 28:1-6, 15-18, 42.*
a) What warning had God given the people through Moses?
b) Discuss the importance of obedience in our walk with God.

DAY 4 *Joel 2:1; Numbers 10:8-9.*
a) Who were to sound the alarm? How? Where? Why?
b) What affect would the sounding of the trumpet have on the people.

DAY 5 *Joel 2:1-11.*
a) What aspects of this invasion would you consider the most frightening?
b) Are there things happening in our land about which we should be very concerned?
c) How is the day of the Lord described (vv. 1-2, 11)?

DAY 6 *Joel 2:11; 1 Thessalonians 5:1-3; 2 Peter 3:10-13.*
a) What day do the New Testament readings point forward to?
b) How do these readings indicate that: 'The person who knows, fears, respects and honours God need not fear the day of the Lord'?
c) Was Joel thinking about this 'day of the Lord' mentioned in the New Testament when he wrote Joel 2:11?

QUESTIONS (contd.)

DAY 7 *Joel 2:12-17.*
    a) In the midst of their troubles what does the Lord invite the people to do?
    b) How were the people to turn back to the Lord?
    c) If we have failed, what truths about God mentioned here should encourage us to turn back to Him in prayer?

NOTES

THE SETTING
Down through the years Israel had constantly been tempted to take God's grace for granted, expecting His blessing and favour to flow as long as the rituals of temple worship continued. They forgot all too easily the warnings which accompanied His covenant.

Joel recognises that the plague is punishment for disobedience and falling away from guidelines given to Moses for the nation. He therefore sees that any relief must come through the leadership of the priests who represent the people to God, and then from the entire nation gathering in humility at the temple.

> People and animals are in a desperate plight.
> Judgment has produced heaviness.
> Joy and gladness are missing in worship.
> Joel leads the way back to God in prayer (1:19).

PROGRESSION IN UNDERSTANDING
Near at hand the prophet sees the havoc caused by a plague of real locusts. Further ahead the plague foreshadows a powerful invading army even more dreadful than the insects. Then this understanding leads him on to see that, even worse than a devastating plague and a plundering army, will come the Day of Judgment when all nations must face God's reckoning.

As no vegetation escapes the locusts, and as Judah will be vulnerable before the approaching enemy, so no one can escape the future Day of the Lord.

POSITIVE ACTION
The call to 'blow the trumpet' in Zion, as a warning to the people, is to summon them for spiritual reasons to come before God with broken hearts (2:13).

CHALLENGE
God looks at our hearts. Do the outward forms of my faith spring from a heart at peace with God?

Who can endure the day of the Lord (2:11)? We can! 'In Christ and by His saving work on the cross we can. Without Christ, no one can' (Goldsmith).

STUDY 7
GOD IS ACTIVE

QUESTIONS

DAY 1 *Joel 2:15-18.*
a) Who were to be involved in seeking God?
b) What were the people to be particularly concerned about in prayer?

DAY 2 *Nehemiah 1.*
a) What similarities exist between Nehemiah's prayer, and the prayer the people in Joel's day were to offer? (Look at its background, passion and content.)
b) What role should emotion have in our prayers?

DAY 3 *Joel 2:18-20a; Deuteronomy 14:2; 1 Samuel 12:22; Ezekiel 39:25.*
a) Why should God be jealous? How does His jealousy differ from human jealousy?
b) What would God do for His people? When would He do this (v. 18a)?

DAY 4 *Joel 2:20b-24.*
a) What theme runs through these verses
b) In whom are the people to rejoice (v. 23) and why?

DAY 5 *Joel 2:21-22.*
a) Who are specially told not to be afraid (v. 22)?
b) Matthew 6:25-34. What lessons are we to learn from God's care for His creation? What are we assured of in Matthew 10:31.

DAY 6 *Joel 2:23-27.*
a) What theme is continued on in these verses?
b) What mistake did the rich fool make in Luke 12:15-21?
c) What did Jesus illustrate by the seed that fell among thorns (Mark 4:18-19)?

DAY 7 *Joel 2:28-32; Acts 2:1-21.*
a) Why did Peter quote these verses from Joel in Acts 2?
b) What in Joel's prophecy still awaits complete fulfilment?

NOTES

THE SETTING
In faithfulness to His people, God silences the puny heathen reproaches as He graciously restores the rains and harvests, meeting the needs of both animal and human population alike. God performs these things in beautiful and bountiful ways. In the future, there would be outstanding events never before witnessed.

A JEALOUS GOD
'God is so concerned for the exclusive honour of His name that He will not allow heathen nations to mock Him by despising and despoiling His land and the holy city of Jerusalem' (Goldsmith).

TRUST ENTERS AND FEAR EXITS
Fear of death, whether through famine, enemy invasion, threatening people or events, can be paralysing, but trust in God brings peace. He alone is trustworthy. Trust in a powerful, caring God brings peace which overflows in joyous testimony.

Steps from fear to faith:
1. Admit that you are afraid, and the cause of the fear.
2. Read and reread verses like Isaiah 43:1. Become confirmed in your assurance that God loves you and watches over you.
3. I Peter 5:7 says, 'Cast (throw) all your anxiety on him because he cares for you'. Be comforted with these words, and also those of Jesus in Matthew 10:31.
4. Joy will rise within, and overflow in praise, as you take your eyes off the fear, and fix them on God.

CHALLENGE FOR TODAY
Take a good look at your church or Christian circle. Can those who do not know God personally see His power at work among you? Is He honoured in your midst? Can the question legitimately be asked, 'Where is your God?'

Let us remember that there is always a need to invite the Holy Spirit to so clothe and empower us that God will be seen in our corporate and private lives.

STUDY 8
GOD STEPS IN

QUESTIONS

DAY 1 *Joel 2:32; Romans 10:9-13.*
a) What promise does Paul repeat from Joel?
b) What does this promise remind us about:
Who can be saved? What two groups of people did Paul mention? How are we saved? When are we are saved? Can we know we are saved? Why can we be saved (Eph. 2:8-9)?

DAY 2 *Joel 2:13; 3:1–3.*
a) How is God's attitude towards His enemies contrasted to that exercised towards His own people?
b) Who does God specially highlight in verse 3? What forms of child abuse exist today?

DAY 3 *Joel 3:4-8.*
Answer whether true or false, and discuss the following statements:
a) God gives the nations freedom to oppress one another without retaliation.
b) The scattered people of God were under His loving surveillance.

DAY 4 *Joel 3:1-3,9-13.*
a) Who will be gathered? And by whom?
b) Why is there a need for judgment? How is the judgment depicted in verse 13 (Isa. 63:1-4)?

DAY 5 *Joel 3:14-16.*
a) What words indicate that this judgment day will be an awesome event?
b) Why would the people of God not be afraid (Ps. 46:1-7)?
c) What comes through believing in the Lord Jesus (John 3:36)?

DAY 6 *Joel 3:17-21; John 3:13-21.*
a) What would be the source of any future blessing for the people of God (vv. 17, 21)? What is said about heaven in Revelation 21:27?

QUESTIONS (contd.)

b) What will happen to those who oppose God (v. 19)?

DAY 7 *Joel 3:1-21.*
Some parts of this chapter we may find hard to understand.
a) How can Christians be encouraged through it today?
b) What in it should make us concerned for those who are not Christians?

NOTES

THE SETTING
God steps into the prophecy of the end times with the reassuring words of Joel 2:32: 'And everyone who calls on the name of the Lord will be saved; for on Mount Zion and in Jerusalem there will be deliverance, as the LORD has said, among the survivors whom the LORD calls'. Chapter three tells more of the way in which the promised deliverance will come.

THE NATIONS
Joel's prophecy spans a long period of time. It foretells the judging and punishment of the nations which have oppressed Judah, and each other. Look up Genesis 22:15-18 and remember God's promise to Abraham, the founding father of Israel and Judah. God promised that from Abraham and his offspring He would raise a mighty and numerous nation through whom all other nations would be blessed. Joel tells of God's call to all nations to gather in the Valley of Jehoshaphat, which is probably a symbolic name, meaning 'The Lord judges'. The harvest of sin is ripe, and wickedness overflows (3:13).

NATIONS ARE PEOPLE
The picture becomes more detailed in 3:14 where we see 'multitudes in the valley of decision'. There are many nations, each made up of large numbers of people. These multitudes are all different, all created by God and known individually to Him. Jesus died for every one of them.

Matthew 9:36-38 and 15:30-31 contain two lovely examples of the love and compassion Christ showed to the crowds. As He talked with them, and worked miracles among them, they saw God at work, and glorified Him. Jesus' cry coming down through the years is for us to open our eyes and see the needs of multitudes, physically, and more especially, spiritually.

GOD OUR REFUGE
The scoffer and the unbeliever may fear the coming Day of the Lord. But the believer, who knows the Judge personally, can rejoice because of His great provision for the care and refreshment of His people (3:18). See also John 3:17-18.

> 'But the LORD will be a refuge for his people, a stronghold for the people of Israel' (Joel 3:16b).

CHALLENGE TODAY
Read again Jesus' words from Matthew 9:36-38. Determine to pray regularly for missionaries and ministers of the gospel as they seek to harvest the lost peoples of the world for the Saviour, before He returns to judge in righteousness.

HABAKKUK and JOEL

STUDY 9
GOD IS GREAT!

QUESTIONS

DAY 1 *Exodus 3:11-15; 6:2-8.*
a) By what name did God make Himself known to the children of Israel, through Moses?
b) Discuss how significant this name of God must have been for Moses.

DAY 2 *Deuteronomy 32:1-4; 33:26-29.*
a) In Moses' songs at the end of his life, who is the object of his praise?
b) What is he really saying about God in the song?

DAY 3 *Psalm 62; 2 Samuel 22:31-34,47.*
a) What is it about the nature of God that David exalts?
b) How is it that David and Moses can praise Him with such assurance?

DAY 4 *Isaiah 6:1-8.*
a) Why did Isaiah feel unclean?
b) What prepared him for service?

DAY 5 *Habakkuk 1:1,12; 2:13; 3:18-19.*
a) List the names Habakkuk gives to God when he addresses Him.
b) In the closing verses of the book how does the prophet view God?

DAY 6 *Revelation 19:1-10.*
a) Who are identified as praising God? What common language do they employ?
b) What command was John given (v. 10)?

DAY 7 *Hebrews 1:1-6; Philippians 2:5-11.*
a) When did Jesus sit down at God's right hand?
b) If you are a Christian, take time to thank God for the gift of salvation He has given you through the death of His Son on the cross.

NOTES

THE SETTING
At creation God saw all He had made, and it was good (Gen. 1:31). Then He rested (Gen. 2:2). Later He raised up a nation from one man, Abraham. He gave this nation a good land and laws to live by, through Moses. He commissioned the nation to be an avenue of His blessing to all other nations. They were to reveal His glory through their behaviour and by His perfect provision for their needs. God was caring, and watched over every individual in the nation. They were set apart to be blessed and to be a blessing to all others around them.

> Abraham knew God as a promise-keeping God.
> Moses found Him to be eternal, and yet ever-present, the great I AM.
> To David, the second king of Israel, God was shepherd, and the rock of his salvation.
> Isaiah, the prophet, saw God in His almighty holiness.
> From the depths of their walk with God, all these were able to testify to His glory, faithfulness and holy justice.

THE PROPHETS
So it is with Habakkuk and Joel. They received messages from God, and grew to know and trust Him by talking and listening to Him. Though their circumstances and messages differed, their findings were similar: that God is in control of nature and nations. They found that God has an ultimate goal for mankind, and that His salvation from the penalty of sin is freely available to all who call on His name. This is broadened in the New Testament where we see that salvation is through faith in the atoning death of Christ for both Jews and Gentiles. God's glory will be known in all the earth, and His Son will be honoured, with every knee bowing at His name.

CONFIDENCE IN GOD
Habakkuk and Joel both found security in the knowledge that God is sovereign over His universe. Joel praised Him for His presence and victory, and Habakkuk for His steadfast reign in the face of coming national collapse.

CHALLENGE
Where do I place my confidence? With whom am I sharing my faith?
Am I making time to talk with and listen to God in whom I have confidence?

ANSWER GUIDE

The following pages contain an Answer Guide. It is recommended that answers to the questions be attempted before turning to this guide. It is only a guide and the answers given should not be treated as exhaustive.

GUIDE TO STUDY 1

DAY 1
a) As a prophet.
b) Violence, unrest, wickedness, etc.
Personal.

DAY 2
a) With concern and prayer to God.
b) To intervene and overthrow the evil doers.
He was seeing no immediate answer to his prayers.

DAY 3
a) Patience and persistence.
b) Keep on praying consistently until the answer comes.
c) Repeat Matthew 7:7 together.

DAY 4
a) God knew where His faithful ones were, and saved them. He allowed the wickedness to prevail for only a limited period.
b) 2 Peter 2:9.

DAY 5
a) God.
b) God was going to raise up a new superpower, the Babylonians. The underlying meaning is that this force will be used to punish the nation of Judah.

DAY 6
a) As fierce, determined and arrogant.
b) Disobedience would bring about an invasion and destruction from a foreign power.
The Babylonians are described as fierce, arrogant, etc.

DAY 7
a) Invincible and masters of their own destiny.
b) God was directing the affairs of the nations.

Encourage group members to read the text in various Bible translations as this will give increased understanding of the books.

GUIDE TO STUDY 2

DAY 1 a) Both were looking for help; both saw no immediate answers to their prayers.
b) He began to meditate on the history of God's dealings with His people.
God was holy and powerful and cared for His people like a shepherd.

DAY 2 a) God.
b) His eternity, sovereignty and holiness.
His holiness.

DAY 3 a) God sees everyone including the wicked.
b) God cannot look on evil without being offended by it or leave it go unpunished.

DAY 4 a) As being wicked, arrogant, idolatrous and delighting in the cruelty of war.
God was allowing them to succeed in their arrogance and wickedness and in their destruction of people more righteous than themselves.
b) They were successful, arrogant and apparently trouble free.
God could easily destroy them so they weren't to be envied.

DAY 5 a) As a lookout, a watchman.
An answer from God to his questions.
b) There is no situation too difficult for prayer. Prayer requires faith and patience.

DAY 6 a) We are not told how long. True prayer waits until God answers.
b) It was for the future and was trustworthy.
c) Ensure that it could be clearly understood by others.

DAY 7 a) The righteous and the nation's arrogant enemies
b) The just (righteous) living by faith.
c) Righteousness can only come through faith in Jesus Christ. As sinners we need the righteousness that God gives.

GUIDE TO STUDY 3

DAY 1 a) By their faith in God.
No; they would be living in a hostile environment.
b) He took refuge in God; he reminded himself who God was, that He was still on His throne.
Personal.

DAY 2 a) An evil or sinful heart.
Probably all, certainly greed and arrogance.
b) They would be overthrown by the people they had conquered. Such rebellions frequently occur, as, for example, in former East European communist bloc countries.

DAY 3 a) They had no scruples or morals and stooped to anything including murder.
Temporal.
b) Through believing in the Lord Jesus and accepting the free gift of eternal life that He offers.

DAY 4 a) God's plan is for all nations to know about Him and worship Him.
b) Through missionary activity. Operation World by Patrick Johnstone reports that we are living in the time of the largest ingathering of people into the Kingdom of God that the world has ever seen.

DAY 5 a) God's cup of judgment would be given them to drink.
b) God's cup of wrath against sin. Jesus suffered in our place.

DAY 6 a) They are only of human creation, unable to help.
b) As God's judgment on those who turn away from truths they should have acknowledged and believed. When we reject what light we have, our darkness will only increase.

DAY 7 a) Awe at His greatness, majesty, power, etc.
b) God is behind world events and is working things out for His glory. The success of evil men is worthless and temporal.

GUIDE TO STUDY 4

DAY 1 a) As a prayer set to music. (The Good News Bible does not include the reference to music.)
'The word shigionoth is believed to be the tempo at which this prayer was originally meant to be sung. The tempo was a strong one, corresponding to the profound emotions raised through the words and concepts of this chapter' (Selwyn Hughes).
b) That God would become active, and once again do great deeds as in the past. He is praying for renewal, or revival. On the basis of God's mercy. Jesus understands our situation.

DAY 2 a) The giving of the law at Sinai.
b) In the Lord Jesus Christ.

DAY 3 a) The Exodus of the children of Israel from Egypt. Joshua's victory (Josh. 10:12-13), etc.
b) On behalf of His own people.

DAY 4 a) It was a decisive, fatal blow to the head; it was a complete victory.
b) It was at the last moment when all hope seemed to have gone.

DAY 5 a) He waited patiently and in faith.
b) Personal.
c) Various possibilities. Example: 'Though crops fail; though I have no job; though everything is going wrong; I trust God to take care of me.

DAY 6 a) This animal would have been sure-footed and swift in difficult terrain. Spiritually Habakkuk wanted to triumph in difficult places. Perhaps there was also the idea of moral elevation. Only God could give him this ability (Phil. 4:13).
b) With Christ in heavenly places. This speaks of the spiritual resources available to a Christians.

DAY 7 a) The first is a cry for help; the second is honest questioning; the third is worship.
b) God had rewarded his faith and patience. Meditation on God's help towards Israel in the past had encouraged him to face the future.

GUIDE TO STUDY 5

DAY 1 a) He was the son of Pethuel. God's word came to him.
b) A plague of locusts, far-reaching in destruction.

DAY 2 a) The elders of the nation.
Reflect on the past and ensure this event was never forgotten about in the future.
b) An event of such magnitude was worthy of record, especially as it had spiritual significance; it highlighted the consequences of sin and the mercy of God.

DAY 3 a) The drunkards.
b) Not as a drunkard! A Christian is to be awake and on guard against Satan's temptations. He or she is to be ready for the coming again of the Lord Jesus.

DAY 4 a) Famine had resulted in the people not being able to bring their offerings to the temple.
b) There is no joy in Joel 1:12 whereas Habakkuk is determined to rejoice whatever happens.

DAY 5 a) Priests, elders, in fact everyone in the land.
b) Mourning, fasting, wearing sackcloth and meeting together in the temple.

DAY 6 a) Earnest, humble, sincere prayer will be rewarded.
b) Opportunity for discussion. Jesus assumes that it will take place.

DAY 7 a) He received God's word and passed it on to the people. He called the people to prayer and fasting.
b) It instructs us about salvation; it teaches, rebukes and directs us.

GUIDE TO STUDY 6

DAY 1 a) As Father.
b) 'my' (v. 13); 'your' (v. 14); 'our' (v. 16).

DAY 2 a) Drought, famine, fire.
Animals, including those wild, were suffering.
b) The day of the Lord.

DAY 3 a) That obedience would bring blessing, and disobedience, curses.
b) Personal.

DAY 4 a) The priests. On trumpets. In Zion. To call on God for help.
b) The people would begin to tremble.

DAY 5 a) Personal.
b) Personal. Some answers could include apathy to the gospel, moral decline, etc.
c) Gloomy, dark, great, dreadful.

DAY 6 a) The great final day of God's day of judgment.
b) The Christian is looking forward to heaven.
c) Perhaps not, but it pointed forward to this final Judgment Day.

DAY 7 a) Return immediately to Him in true repentance.
b) Wholeheartedly; it wasn't to be something superficial.
c) His compassion and love, etc.

GUIDE TO STUDY 7

DAY 1 a) Everyone, including the little children.
b) The glory of God. People were despising them; it did not appear as if God was doing anything to help them.

DAY 2 a) Both were born out of a background of trouble and disgrace; both were passionate involving weeping and fasting; both included confession and repentance; both were concerned for God's reputation and glory.
b) Personal. When we are desperate about something we will not be tame or polite in our expressions before God.

DAY 3 a) They were His people whom he had specially chosen; it was His land, promised to His chosen people from Abraham onwards. God was committed to His people to care for them among the surrounding nations. God's jealousy stems from His pure love for the people and His land, while human jealousy is sinful and one-sided.
b) Take pity on them, provide for them and destroy the army (most likely the locusts).
After repentance and earnest prayer.

DAY 4 a) The theme of abundant provision and joy.
b) In the Lord; it was He who had given them this provision.

DAY 5 a) The land and the animals.
b) God's active interest in and provision for His creation is a clear sign that He will provide for His children. Matthew 10:31 assures us of our value in God's sight.

DAY 6 a) The wonderful things that God will do for His people.
b) He forgot who had given him his harvest. His attention was focused only on material things to the detriment of spiritual riches.
c) Unless we are careful, prosperity can harm us spiritually.

DAY 7 a) He realised that Joel's prophecy about the Holy Spirit had been fulfilled at Pentecost.
b) The coming great day of the Lord, or judgment, still has to take place.

GUIDE TO STUDY 8

DAY 1
a) 'Everyone who calls on the name of the Lord will be saved.'
b) Everyone. Paul mentions Jews and Gentiles.
By calling on the Lord.
When we call on the Lord.
Yes; this is God's promise to all who call.
Through grace alone; salvation is the gift of God.

DAY 2
a) God enters into judgment with the nations; He exercised compassion and kindness towards His own people.
b) The abuse suffered by children. Many kinds of abuse: think of street children, child soldiers, sexual abuse, etc. Many millions of children are suffering worldwide today.

DAY 3
a) False.
b) True.

DAY 4
a) All the nations will be gathered by God.
b) Because wickedness has increased to its full extent.
As a trampling of grapes in a winepress.

DAY 5
a) Creation is in commotion and the Lord roaring as a lion.
b) God would be their refuge and stronghold.
c) Escape from God's wrath to come.

DAY 6
a) Holiness and God dwelling in their midst.
Nothing impure will enter heaven; only believers will be there.
b) They will be judged; their country would be desolate.

DAY 7
a) God watches over His children; evil will finally be overthrown, etc.
b) They will be judged by God; God sees their behaviour, etc.

GUIDE TO STUDY 9

DAY 1 a) I AM. Jehovah. (The Lord, as in 3:15 = YAHWEH, or Jehovah.)
b) Moses' faith in God was confirmed. He realised that God is eternal, from everlasting to everlasting.

DAY 2 a) God.
b) He is praising God as trustworthy, eternal, and as a refuge for His people.

DAY 3 a) David is confident in God's rocklike stability and reliability.
b) Both had very intimate and personal experiences of God and His faithfulness.

DAY 4 a) He was confronted by the holiness of God. His own righteousness was as uncleanness.
b) The cleansing of his lips. He had specifically confessed the uncleanness of his words, and God cleansed the area of confessed sin. See 1 John 1:9.

DAY 5 a) Lord, God, Holy One, Rock, Lord Almighty, Saviour, Sovereign Lord (all found in the New International Version).
b) Habakkuk has come to see God as his Saviour, and as the reigning monarch over the affairs of all.

DAY 6 a) A great multitude; the elders and living creatures.
NIV has 'Hallelujah'.
b) He was to worship God alone.

DAY 7 a) After He had made atonement for our sins (Heb. 1:3).
b) Personal.

THE WORD WORLDWIDE

We first heard of WORD WORLDWIDE over 20 years ago when Marie Dinnen, its founder, shared excitedly about the wonderful way ministry to a needy woman had exploded to touch many lives. It was great to see the Word of God being made central in the lives of thousands of men and women, then the life changing effects that resulted when they applied the Word into their circumstances. Over the years the vision for WORD WORLDWIDE has not dimmed in the hearts of those who are involved in this ministry. God is still at work through His Word and in today's self-seeking society, the Word is even more relevant to those who desire true meaning and purpose in life. WORD WORLDWIDE is a ministry of WEC International, an interdenominational missionary society, whose sole purpose for existence is to see Christ known, loved and worshipped by all, particularly those who have yet to hear of His wonderful name. This ministry is a vital part of our work and we warmly recommend the WORD WORLDWIDE 'Geared for Growth' Bible studies to you. We know that as you study His Word you will be enriched in your personal walk with Christ. It is our hope that as you are blessed through these studies, you will find opportunities to help others find a personal relationship with Jesus. As a mission we would encourage you to work with us to make Christ known to the ends of the earth.

Stewart and Jean Moulds – British Directors, **WEC International.**

A full list of over 50 'Geared for Growth' studies can be obtained from:

ENGLAND John and Ann Edwards
5 Louvain Terrace, Hetton-le Hole, Tyne & Wear, DH5 9PP
Tel. 0191 5262803 Email: rhysjohn.edwards@virgin.net

IRELAND Steffney Preston
33 Harcourts Hill, Portadown, Craigavon, N. Ireland, BT62 3RE
Tel. 028 3833 7844 Email: sa.preston@talk21.com

SCOTLAND Margaret Halliday
10 Douglas Drive, Newton Mearns, Glasgow, G77 6HR
Tel. 0141 639 8695• Email: m.halliday@ntlworld.com

WALES William and Eirian Edwards
Penlan Uchaf, Carmarthen Road, Kidwelly, Carms., SA17 5AF
Tel. 01554 890423 Email: Penlan.uchaf@farming.co.uk

UK CO-ORDINATOR
Anne Jenkins, 2 Windermere Road, Carnforth, Lancs., LA5 9AR
Tel. 01524 734797 Email: anne@jenkins.abelgratis.com

www.wordworldwide.org.uk

Christian Focus Publications publishes biblically-accurate books for adults and children. The books in the adult range are published in three imprints.

Christian Heritage contains classic writings from the past.

Christian Focus contains popular works including biographies, commentaries, doctrine, and Christian living.

Mentor focuses on books written at a level suitable for Bible College and seminary students, pastors, and others; the imprint includes commentaries, doctrinal studies, examination of current issues, and church history.

For a free catalogue of all our titles, please write to the address below.

ISBN 0 90806 751 8

Copyright © WEC International

Published in 2002 by
Christian Focus Publications, Geanies House,
Fearn, Ross-shire, IV20 ITW, Scotland
and
WEC International, Bulstrode, Oxford Road,
Gerrards Cross, Bucks , SL9 8SZ

www.christianfocus.com

Cover design by Alister MacInnes

Printed and bound by Bell and Bain